COMPACTING AND THE SCHOOLWIDE ENRICHMENT MODEL

Compacting is one of the major components of the Schoolwide Enrichment Model **(SEM)**, our widely implemented enrichment program used with academically gifted and talented students and for all students in schools using a theme related to talent development, enrichment, or creativity (Renzulli & Reis, 2014).

The Schoolwide Enrichment Model
Joseph S. Renzulli & Sally M. Reis

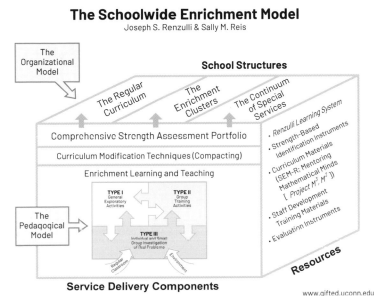

www.gifted.uconn.edu

FIGURE 1. The Schoolwide Enrichment Model.

The SEM **(see Figure 1)** is implemented in thousands of school districts across the country and the world. In the SEM, enriched learning experiences and higher learning standards are provided for all children through developing talents; providing a broad range of advanced-level, in-depth enrichment experiences for high-potential and academically talented students; and follow-up exploratory and more intense learning for students based on their developing interests. The SEM emphasizes engagement and the use of enjoyable and challenging learning experiences that are constructed around students' interests, learning styles, and expression/product styles.

3 STEPS FOR IMPLEMENTING CURRICULUM COMPACTING

Curriculum compacting involves (Reis, Renzulli, & Burns, 2016):

1
Defining the goals and learning outcomes of a particular content area or unit of instruction.

2
Determining and documenting the students who have already mastered most or all of a specified set of learning outcomes.

3
Providing replacement strategies for material already mastered through the use of instructional options that enable a more challenging, engaging, interesting, and productive use of the student's time.

Teachers who use compacting streamline curriculum through a practical, step-by-step approach, learn the skills required to modify curriculum and the techniques for pretesting students, and prepare enrichment and/or acceleration options based on individual areas of interest.

THE COMPACTOR FORM

The curriculum compacting process is easily introduced through the use of the Compactor Form (see Figure 2 for an example of a completed form).

Individual Education Program Guide The Compactor		
Student Name(s): Nick Jackson	Grade: 4	School: San Jose Elementary School
Participating Teachers:		
Name It	**Prove It**	**Change It**
Curriculum Area Name the subject area, unit, chapter, or learning standards that are the focus for compacting.	**Assessment** List the assessment tools and related data that indicate student strengths and interests. List the preassesment data and the learning standards that have not yet been mastered.	**Enrichment/Acceleration Plans** Briefly describe the strategies used to ensure mastery of the learning standards that have not been mastered. Name the enrichment or acceleration tasks that will be substituted for the compacted curriculum.
Math ♦ Nick was a second grader in 2012–2013. He skipped third grade, but tested extremely high on the end-of-third-grade math benchmark at the end of his second grade year. **Reading** ♦ Nick's testing shows comprehension at a high school level. He also reads very accurately and fluently. **Spelling** ♦ All students are given the opportunity to compact spelling on a weekly basis.	**Math** ♦ In August of this year, he was given the end-of-fourth-grade district benchmark and scored 90%. ♦ Nick will take a pretest (end-of-unit test in the book) for each unit covered this year. If he shows mastery (85% +), then we will compact that unit. If he shows less than 85% on any unit or topic within a unit, then he will work with the class on that specific area. As he will likely compact most units, pretests will be given during the final testing period for the previous unit. Separate times can be arranged as necessary. **Reading** ♦ He will be asked to complete comprehension tests using the Accelerated Reader program to ensure understanding of the material. Observation of group discussions and collection of literature circle material will also show proficiency in this area. **Spelling** ♦ Each Monday, students are given a pretest on the weekly spelling list. Any student who scores 80%–100% correct is given the opportunity to compact. These pretests measure proficiency with the basic spelling lists.	**Math** ♦ Subject matter acceleration is not an option in this school, so it is likely he will need the math curriculum compacted. ♦ Nick has expressed interested in working on a Type III project that culminates in a presentation at the annual Student to Student conference in April. Our school does not have a resource teacher/GATE teacher, but a parent volunteer and I will guide him through this project. He will be given time to work on this during time saved by compacting. **Reading** ♦ Students are ability grouped for reading instruction. Within these groups, they work in small groups to complete many of the instructional activities. Nick will be grouped with other advanced readers and given higher level books to read and discuss. The advanced readers will tackle more difficult books. They will discuss and complete literature circle packets that include higher level thinking topics and questions. Students in the group will get to choose their books from a given group, with each student having input. **Spelling** ♦ Students who score 80%–100% on the pretest will be given the chance to create their own spelling list for the week. The lists must have 15 words and must include any words that they missed on the original list. Students with "challenge lists" pair up and test each other during spelling test time.

FIGURE 2. Sample completed Compactor. From *Curriculum Compacting: A Guide to Differentiating Curriculum and Instruction Through Enrichment and Acceleration* (2nd ed., pp. 159–160), by S. M. Reis, J. S. Renzulli, and D. E. Burns, 2016, Waco, TX: Prufrock Press. Copyright 2016 by Prufrock Press. Reprinted with permission.

THE COMPACTOR FORM, Continued.

Name It: Completing the First Column of the Compactor

- Name the content areas being considered for compacting.
- Cite information that indicates that the student is a good candidate for compacting. For example:

> "John's achievement test score in math (99th percentile) indicates curriculum compacting is necessary."

> "Tamara's grades in English have been A's for the last 4 years."

> "Liza's instructional reading level is 4 years above her grade placement."

> In each of these cases, the teacher provided evidence of above-average ability in the subject area. Information from test scores, classroom behaviors, and notes on performance assessment can also be used to document curriculum strength.

- Provide information about the objective(s) being considered for compacting. For example:

> "John will be pretested on the math computation objectives in the fourth-grade math program."

> "Writing objectives will be considered for compacting for Danni, who is writing several years above grade level."

> "It is likely that Liza can be compacted from vocabulary and comprehension objectives for this and the next grade level."

> *All* possible objectives or curricular areas to be considered for compacting do not need to be identified during the first week of the school year. The process will likely start slowly with one student or in one content area. As the teacher and students become more proficient with the process, additional objectives for compacting will be identified and additional notes can be added in the remaining space in Column One.

Prove It: Completing the Second Column of the Compactor

- Document the objectives and pretest results. Indicate which objectives were pretested. The use of codes, numbered objectives, or references to objectives is appropriate. The parent or teacher who sees the Compactor should be able to understand the extent of the pretest and the specific skills or content objectives tested. Record this information as succinctly as possible; use scanned copies of the assessments, tests, or objectives on an electronic compactor form. Be precise about which objectives need to be mastered by documenting the scores of *each* objective that should be compacted.
- Document *how* the specific objectives will be achieved. For example, if a student has shown mastery of seven of the 10 objectives in a unit, the teacher must decide how to provide instruction in the remaining three objectives. The teacher may require that the student participate with the rest of the class, learn through an individual tutorial, or become responsible for independent mastery.
- Document how much time has been saved for enrichment or acceleration activities and what is being eliminated from the classroom curriculum as a result of mastery of tested objectives. If, for example, spelling pretests indicate that a student has mastery of six of the next eight units in the spelling curriculum, the writer might indicate the dates, the times of day, or the days of the week when the six units are to be taught.

Change It: Completing the Third Column of the Compactor

- Document how time provided by the compacting process is to be spent through enrichment/acceleration.
- Enhance and add to this column as more options emerge based on increased knowledge of students' strengths.

ALTERNATIVES TO THE COMPACTOR FORM

Using or adapting the Compactor is a decision that can and should be made by individual teachers or a committee of teachers within the school or district. The form enables teachers to document all instances of change from the regular curriculum. In states that have a mandate for gifted education, the Compactor might also be used to reduce some of the paperwork required for students who are receiving special, state-funded services. In many of these cases, gifted education is classified under the special education program and the due process procedures that are required; the Compactor has often been used as a substitute for the Individual Education Plan **(IEP)**.

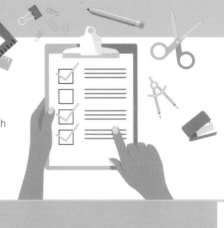

The Compactor documents all instances of curricular modification; it can easily be used to record the assessment information that led to compacting. It will also provide information about the enrichment or acceleration options that were offered to students who took advantage of the compacting procedure.

Some teachers prefer to keep track of students' pretest scores using a matrix in which every student is listed, as are skills and content areas that must be mastered. Teachers might use checklists or matrices that are provided with their district curriculum maps or adapt existing forms for their own purposes. Others prefer to keep records for each student in the class. The latter approach can also be combined with an individual student record and a contract that describes required assignments and optional activities.

3 STRATEGIES FOR RECORD KEEPING AND DOCUMENTATION

You can choose to use the Compactor form as it is, modify it, or use your own recordkeeping devices, but we strongly recommend documentation occur:

1
During parent-teacher conferences or with teachers in subsequent grade levels, which can support teachers in the continued use of compacting.

2
When students move and transfer to a new school system so that a student does not repeat inappropriate grade-level material, as the new school will be able to identify the student's strengths without repeating testing procedures.

3
When teachers are using the compacting process in a less-than-supportive situation, as through attempts to define, preassess, and document learning objectives, they can better explain why some students can be excused from selected instruction or practice.

Why Provide Documentation?: An Example

Consider a primary grade teacher who has been attempting to compact curriculum for her precocious readers during the last 2 years. Her efforts have been thwarted several times by the district's reading supervisor, who believes that repetition builds mastery. When the teacher asked for preassessment strategies that were associated with the district's reading series, the supervisor told her that the pretests were not to be used and that the posttests were only to be given to the class as a large group after finishing each of the two required readers for their grade level. Teachers in the district were told to teach the reading series to the whole group and that no student should be compacted or allowed to use an out-of-level reading.

The situation was frustrating, and finally, the teacher located a norm-referenced, diagnostic reading test that gave her the backup she needed to confront the supervisor about the policy of large-group instruction in the district's reading program. Armed with the objectives for the grade-level reading program and a set of test scores from the diagnostic reading test, the teacher called a conference with the reading supervisor and her principal. As she expected, when she showed the supervisor the actual test scores for able readers in her classroom and suggested that these students were wasting their time by participating in needless instruction and practice, the reading director supported compacting for this group.

WHAT THE RESEARCH SAYS ABOUT CURRICULUM COMPACTING

Dozens of research studies have been conducted on curriculum compacting, some of which are doctoral dissertations, and many that have been case studies of successful use of compacting.

Findings

A national study completed at the National Research Center on the Gifted and Talented (Reis et al., 1993) examined the use of curriculum compacting with students from a wide variety of school districts.

Participants included 465 grade 2–6 classroom teachers from 27 school districts throughout the country. Several urban schools were included, including a magnet school for Hispanic students. Classroom teachers were randomly assigned to participate in either the treatment (implemented compacting) or the control group (continued with normal teaching practices). The most important finding from this research might be described as the more-for-less finding:

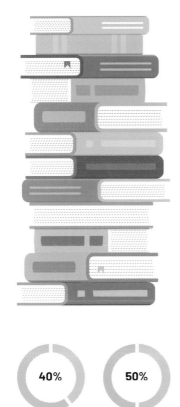

Approximately **40%–50%** of traditional classroom material was compacted for targeted students in one or more content areas. When teachers eliminated as much as 50% of regular curricular activities for targeted students, no differences were observed in posttest achievement scores between treatment and control groups in math concepts, math computation, social studies, and spelling.

In science, students who had **40%–50%** of their curriculum eliminated actually scored significantly higher on science achievement posttests than their peers in the control group. And students whose curriculum was compacted in mathematics scored significantly higher than their peers in the control group on the math concepts posttest.

40%   **50%**

In another study (Baum, Renzulli, & Hébert, 1995), teachers were asked to use both curriculum compacting and self-selected Type III enrichment projects based on students' interests as a systematic intervention for a diverse group of underachieving talented students. Using compacting and Type III enrichment, underachievement was reversed in the majority of students. The use of compacting and replacement of high-interest projects specifically targeted student strengths and interests to cause this reversal.

These findings clearly point out the benefits of curriculum compacting as far as standard achievement is concerned. Analyses of data related to replacement activities also indicated that students viewed these activities as more challenging than standard material.

" What the research says is that curriculum compacting works! "

WHY COMPACT CURRICULUM?

Curriculum compacting enables both curriculum and instruction to be paced in response to students' individual needs. Most academically talented students learn more quickly than others of their age and require a more accelerated pace of instruction than their peers. Sometimes, these learners need a chance to think more deeply about one aspect of a lesson than others, as they may, at certain times and under certain circumstances, become passionately engaged with a topic or experience burning desires to thoroughly understand some aspect of the curriculum.

> " Curriculum compacting helps teachers escalate and increase the challenge for students who absolutely need to engage with some level of difficulty. "

Higher challenge is critical for this group of students because the greatest contributor to the underachievement of gifted and talented students is the lack of challenge that they encounter in elementary and middle school.

High-potential and academically talented learners should grapple with curriculum, instruction, and the completion of products that are complex, challenging, and in-depth. Some students will need support and direction to tackle more difficult work, while other academically talented students may actually need less direction from their teachers, depending on the level of tasks and type of work. The learners who may be able to work more independently are often those with intense interests or the capacity to identify interests that they may want to pursue.

References

Assouline, S., Colangelo, N., VanTassel-Baska, J., & Lupkowski-Shoplik, A. (Eds.). (2015). *A nation empowered: Evidence trumps the excuses that hold back America's brightest students* (Vol. 2). Iowa City: University of Iowa, The Connie Belin & Jacqueline N. Blank International Center for Gifted Education and Talent Development.

Baum, S. M., Renzulli, J. S., & Hébert, T. P. (1995). Reversing underachievement: Creative productivity as a systematic intervention. *Gifted Child Quarterly, 39,* 224–235.

Firmender, J. M., Reis S. M., & Sweeny, S. M. (2013). Reading comprehension and fluency levels ranges across diverse classrooms: The need for differentiated reading instruction and content. *Gifted Child Quarterly, 57,* 3–14.

Reis, S. M., Renzulli, J. S., & Burns, D. E. (2016). *Curriculum compacting: A guide to differentiating curriculum and instruction through enrichment and acceleration* (2nd ed.). Waco, TX: Prufrock Press.

Reis, S. M., Westberg, K. L., Kulikowich, J., Calliard, F., Hébert, T., Purcell, J. H., . . . & Plucker, J. (1993). *Why not let high ability students start school in January? The curriculum compacting study* (RM93106). Storrs: University of Connecticut, The National Research Center on the Gifted and Talented.

Renzulli, J. S., & Reis, S. M. (2014). *The schoolwide enrichment model: A how-to guide for talent development* (3rd ed.). Waco, TX: Prufrock Press.

About the Authors

Sally M. Reis, Ph.D., just completed a 6-year term as the Vice Provost for Academic Affairs at the University of Connecticut. She is a Board of Trustees Distinguished Professor, and a Teaching Fellow in Educational Psychology at the University of Connecticut. She currently holds the Letitia Neag Chair in Educational Psychology.

Joseph S. Renzulli, Ed.D., is a long-time Board of Trustees Distinguished Professor and member of the Department of Educational Psychology at UConn, is a winner of the McGraw Hill Education Prize, and served as the Director of the National Research Center on the Gifted and Talented for more than two decades.

$12.95 US

Copyright ©2018, Prufrock Press Inc.

Edited by Katy McDowall

Layout design by Allegra Denbo

No part of this guide may be reproduced without written permission from the publisher. Visit https://www.prufrock.com/permissions.aspx.

Please visit our website at https://www.prufrock.com.

Printed in the USA

PRUFROCK PRESS INC.™

ISBN-13: 978-1-61821-788-2

51295

9 781618 217882

EDUCATOR'S
QUICK REFERENCE GUIDE
to curriculum compacting

by Sally M. Reis, Ph.D., and Joseph S. Renzulli, Ed.D.

WHAT IS CURRICULUM COMPACTING?

CURRICULUM COMPACTING is a research-based common-sense differentiation strategy, based on the philosophy that all students deserve to make continuous progress learning in school.

Students also deserve to learn new content and be exposed to big ideas and concepts that extend their thinking. All students should be able to continually increase their talents, skills, and knowledge (e.g., students who enter third grade reading at a sixth-grade level deserve the opportunity to enter fourth grade reading at least at a seventh-grade level). But this only happens when teachers are innovative, flexible, and reflective, and when they commit to the notion of instruction that responds to students' needs and the importance of continuous progress in learning for all students.

Curriculum compacting is a differentiation strategy that incorporates
1. content,
2. process,
3. products,
4. classroom management, and
5. teachers' personal commitment to accommodating individual and small-group differences, based on Renzulli's five dimensions of differentiation.

Compacting enables teachers at all grades, in many subject areas, to address the demand for more challenging learning experiences designed to help all students achieve at high levels and realize their potential.

HOW DOES COMPACTING HELP TALENTED STUDENTS?

Academically talented students need time to think, reflect on, understand, and experience challenging content. They also need to learn to expend effort and employ study skills to enable them to achieve at increasingly higher levels than they previously believed possible. These types of opportunities should be made available to all students, but we believe curriculum compacting *must* be implemented for high-potential and gifted learners as a minimum level of service to provide them with academic challenge in school. Indeed, good instruction for talented and high-potential learners can and should begin with the compacting process.

Student Behaviors That Suggest That Compacting Is Necessary

Consistently finishes tasks quickly		Asks for simple enrichment—activities, online work, puzzles, kits, etc.	
	Completes reading assignments first in the class		Brings in outside reading material to use in class
Often daydreams or appears bored in class		Appears bored during instruction time	
Achieves high test scores consistently		Creates diversions in class and may misbehave or ask for attention	
	Has consistently high performance in one or more academic areas	Is sought after by other students for assistance	
Asks questions that indicate advanced familiarity with material		Uses vocabulary and verbal expression in advance of grade level	
	Expresses interest in pursuing alternate or advanced topics		

Note. From Reis, Renzulli, & Burns, 2016. Reprinted with permission.

7 REASONS TO COMPACT CURRICULUM

1

It offers high-potential and talented students instruction that identifies and eliminates curriculum that students already know. They won't have to wait for other students to learn the content they have already mastered. Our research shows that most advanced learners are regularly assigned work that they have already mastered. They have to wait for peers to catch up, rather than learning something new, leading to boredom that can be prevented if students have their content knowledge assessed before they start any new work.

2

It stops students from being assigned more of the same work. "Glad that you did so well on that math pretest—here are 80 more advanced problems" is the fastest way to kill the desire and motivation to demonstrate competency and show teachers what a student knows.

3

It enables students to have opportunities for independence and choice in their learning. It should also give them time to learn from their teachers and interact with other students at a similar level of learning potential or achievement. These students need to be challenged and deserve enriching and interesting work, not doing more of the same or simply being assigned more challenging work in areas not of interest to the students.

4

It gives students opportunities to pursue their interests and become independent learners, avoiding underachievement and maintaining high achievement. Our research has found that opportunities for students to become immersed in enrichment learning make a difference in their education and subsequent lives and can help to avoid underachievement. For example, we and our colleagues have studied students who were underachieving in school; these students worked with mentors who supported their completion of a self-selected Type III independent study that helped to reverse their underachievement.

5

It helps teachers address the very broad range of achievement in their classrooms. One of our studies (Firmender, Reis, & Sweeny, 2013) examined the range of reading fluency and comprehension scores of more than 1,000 students in five diverse elementary schools, including a gifted and talented magnet school. We found a remarkably large range in reading comprehension across all schools. For example, the reading level range was 9.2 grade levels in grade 3, 11.3 in grade 4, and 11.6 in grade 5. These ranges of reading achievement levels across all students strongly illustrate the need for teachers to compact content and instruction so all students can make continuous progress.

6

It works best with some form of grouping, but it is absolutely necessary to challenge high-potential and talented students who are educated in every heterogeneous group of students. Compacting works best when a group of high-achieving students is intentionally placed in an otherwise heterogeneous classroom with a teacher who has both the skills and willingness to provide appropriate challenges for these students. Cluster grouping is a popular and often recommended strategy for meeting the needs of high-achieving students in the regular classroom, and is often implemented with compacting.

7

It can be embedded into many other types of programs and services for gifted and talented students (e.g., cluster grouping). Several methods exist for teachers to combine differentiation strategies. Suggestions for how to do this effectively are made throughout this guide, but compacting can be implemented in most enrichment and acceleration programs. In fact, compacting is one of the research-proven acceleration strategies included in the well-known book on acceleration, *A Nation Empowered* (Assouline, Colangelo, VanTassel-Baska, & Lupkowski-Shoplik, 2015).